Lost Gems

SET IN SOUL

This Journal Belongs To

_____

Dedicated To The Love I Will Never Let Go Of.
I Know You Are With Me.
I Know You Are Home.

Table Of Contents

How To Use This Journal

Dealing with the loss of a loved one is never easy. Trying to find a way to cope with the news and the reality that you physically will not see your loved one again has broken you apart inside. How do you cope? How do you move on? What do you do now? While the loss of a loved one does not necessarily get easier, it does become something you can live with. This journal will help you to deal with unfinished love. Grieving is an expression of hurt love. Whether your loved one transitioned over too soon by taking their own life, or by losing their life due to a disease, a tragic event or even a broken heart, this journal will aid you in healing and moving forward. You must be in a place where you want to heal in order to actually heal. While your loved one will never come back, know that they are not far. With God, they are home. This Lost Gems journal is unlike any other form of healing. This journal is a place where you will write to your loved one directly. Each day is an opportunity to communicate your thoughts. This is where you will let your tears tell your thoughts. This is where you will set your secrets free with what you always wanted to tell your loved one. In this journal, the term "transitioned over" is used to replace "passed away" as we believe that all our loved ones transition into a new life with God. It is suggested that you write in this journal every morning and night. Jot down your thoughts at any time in the freestyling sections. The daily prompts are there to guide your thoughts and feelings. Some days you may feel the same as the last few days, and there will be some days you may feel completely different. Leave everything you need to say on the page. Answer the questions as if you are talking to the one you lost. The process of grieving is not one you should go through alone, so with the help of this journal you are going to get through this with God and the one you lost in your heart. This process is a gentle process. It is not a feel-better-overnight process. Everyone grieves differently. Regardless of the stage you are in, this journal will serve as an aid outside of prayer to move forward.

There are three sections in this journal. Each section covers sixty days that will get you through releasing, coping and moving forward. It is highly suggested that you use this journal in conjunction with your Bible and prayer time. The motivational quotes found throughout this journal are there to help keep your spirits up. Answer the periodic questions that come up throughout the pages as freely as you like. Accepting their transition and moving forward with your life does not mean you are leaving your loved one behind. It simply means you are taking all the gems they placed in your heart with you everywhere you go. This is your time to let it all out and let your loved one know that they are your gem.

Grieving Thoughts

Grieving Thoughts

Who Transitioned Over:

You Transitioned Over On (Write The Date):

You Were (Write Where They Were When They Transitioned Over):

You Died Of:

On The Day You Transitioned Over, These Things Were Happening:

Grieving Thoughts

On The Day You Transitioned Over, I Was:

I Found Out You Transitioned Over (Write How):

Your Death Was (Write Whether It Was Forseen Or UnForseen):

Did They Commit Suicide?

If Yes To The Previous Question, Do You Know Why?

Grieving Thoughts

We Met (Write The Details):

Your Favorite Food Was:

Your Favorite Song Was:

Your Favorite Movie Was:

You Always Liked To Wear:

Grieving Thoughts

You Loved Saying:

Your Weirdest Habit:

Your Favorite Position To Lay In:

The Craziest Story You've Ever Told:

You Were Known For:

Grieving Thoughts

It No Longer Feels The Same (Write What Doesn't Feel The Same):

It No Longer Looks The Same (Write What Doesn't Look The Same):

I Currently Have To:

My Current Support System:

My Nickname For You Was:

Grieving Thoughts

You Were So Close To:

Your Relationship To Me Was:

I Know You Would Have Wanted Me To:

How Everyone Acted After You Transitioned Over Helped Me:

How Everyone Acted After You Transitioned Over Hurt Me:

Grieving Thoughts

After You Transitioned Over, It Was Hard Dealing With:

I Stayed Away Because (If This Applies):

I Forgive You For:

I Hated How:

I Loved How:

Grieving Thoughts

You Were The Best At:

I Would Describe You To Be:

I Remember When You Said:

Every Morning I Feel:

Every Night I Feel:

Grieving Thoughts

Ever Since You've Transitioned Over, I Have:

In The Past When I Have Thought Of You, I Would Think:

Some Dreams I Have Had Of You:

The Greatest Lesson I've Learned From You:

The Greatest Lesson I've Taken Away Since Your Passing:

Grieving Thoughts

This Is What I Want To Say To You For The Last Time:

What I Feel Like I Lost In You:

I Remember The Time:

I Wish You Saw:

I Wish We Did:

Grieving Thoughts

We Were Suppose To:

Some Of My Favorite Memories Of Us:

I Am So Frustrated About:

Even Though I Didn't Cause Your Death, I Feel Guilty About (If Applicable):

What I Really Need Right Now:

Grieving Thoughts

What You Didn't Understand About Me:

What I Wish I Could Have Told You:

After You've Transitioned Over, I've Decided To:

After You've Transitioned Over, I Have Picked Up:

After You've Transitioned Over, I Have Stopped:

Grieving Thoughts

Silence Makes Me Feel:

Noise Makes Me Feel:

I Now Reevaluate:

Losing You Showed Me:

Losing You Changed Me:

Grieving Thoughts

You Left Behind:

Our Love (Write Whether It Was An Unconditional Love Or A Love/Hate Relationship):

You Impacted My Life By:

What We Shared In Common:

I Don't Understand Why I:

Grieving Thoughts

I've Been Told I Need To:

Nobody Knows:

What Makes Losing You So Difficult?

I Had Comfort In Knowing:

This Is A Wake Up Call For Me:

Grieving Thoughts

It's Hard For Me To Accept That:

I Feel Like I No Longer Have:

What I Cherish We Did Together:

What I Remember Most:

What I Will Always Carry With Me:

Grieving Thoughts

Everyday I Gain Strength In Knowing:

You Brought Me Joy When You Would:

The Best Decision I Believe You've Made In Your Life:

I'm Glad I Was Able To Be A Part Of (Write Some Life Events You Were A Part Of):

I Wish I Could Have Been A Part Of (Write Some Life Events You Wish You Could Have Been A Part Of):

Grieving Thoughts

Events In My Life That You Have Helped Me With:

I Believe Your Purpose In My Life Was:

I Am A Better Person Because:

I Can Move On Knowing:

I Am Releasing:

Grieving Thoughts

I Don't Know Why But:

A Prayer I Hold Close To My Heart:

I Am Grateful For:

I Am Choosing:

I Will Honor You:

THE FIRST 60 DAYS:

I Am Releasing

I Am Releasing

Date: I Am Feeling:

Morning Thoughts

I Want: Today's Declaration:

I Really Miss: I Am Allowing Myself Time To:

I Believe: I Laid Awake/Fell Asleep Last Night
                                          Thinking:

Nightly Thoughts

Today My Loss Felt: To Get My Mind Off Of My Loss, I
                                          Did:

I Am Starting To: Today God Comforted Me By:

I'm Really Surprised That I: Helpful Things That Have Been Done
                                          And/Or Said To Help Me Heal:

I Am Releasing

Date: I Am Feeling:

Morning Thoughts

I Want: Today's Declaration:

I Really Miss: I Am Allowing Myself Time To:

I Believe: I Laid Awake/Fell Asleep Last Night
                                         Thinking:

Nightly Thoughts

Today My Loss Felt: To Get My Mind Off Of My Loss, I
                                         Did:

I Am Starting To: Today God Comforted Me By:

I'm Really Surprised That I: Helpful Things That Have Been Done
                                         And/Or Said To Help Me Heal:

I Am Releasing

Date: I Am Feeling:

Morning Thoughts

I Want: Today's Declaration:

I Really Miss: I Am Allowing Myself Time To:

I Believe: I Laid Awake/Fell Asleep Last Night
                                         Thinking:

Nightly Thoughts

Today My Loss Felt: To Get My Mind Off Of My Loss, I
                                         Did:

I Am Starting To: Today God Comforted Me By:

I'm Really Surprised That I: Helpful Things That Have Been Done
                                         And/Or Said To Help Me Heal:

I will always love you.

Everything I've needed to say, I've said with tears.

To not feel overwhelmed about losing you, I....

I Am Releasing

Date: I Am Feeling:

Morning Thoughts

I Want: Today's Declaration:

I Really Miss: I Am Allowing Myself Time To:

I Believe: I Laid Awake/Fell Asleep Last Night Thinking:

Nightly Thoughts

Today My Loss Felt: To Get My Mind Off Of My Loss, I Did:

I Am Starting To: Today God Comforted Me By:

I'm Really Surprised That I: Helpful Things That Have Been Done And/Or Said To Help Me Heal:

I Am Releasing

Date: I Am Feeling:

Morning Thoughts

I Want: Today's Declaration:

I Really Miss: I Am Allowing Myself Time To:

I Believe: I Laid Awake/Fell Asleep Last Night
                                         Thinking:

Nightly Thoughts

Today My Loss Felt: To Get My Mind Off Of My Loss, I
                                         Did:

I Am Starting To: Today God Comforted Me By:

I'm Really Surprised That I: Helpful Things That Have Been Done
                                         And/Or Said To Help Me Heal:

I Am Releasing

Date: I Am Feeling:

Morning Thoughts

I Want: Today's Declaration:

I Really Miss: I Am Allowing Myself Time To:

I Believe: I Laid Awake/Fell Asleep Last Night
                                         Thinking:

Nightly Thoughts

Today My Loss Felt: To Get My Mind Off Of My Loss, I
                                         Did:

I Am Starting To: Today God Comforted Me By:

I'm Really Surprised That I: Helpful Things That Have Been Done
                                         And/Or Said To Help Me Heal:

Before you transitioned over, I know you were....

I miss you
everyday.

Grieving Thoughts

I Am Releasing

Date: I Am Feeling:

Morning Thoughts

I Want: Today's Declaration:

I Really Miss: I Am Allowing Myself Time To:

I Believe: I Laid Awake/Fell Asleep Last Night
                                        Thinking:

Nightly Thoughts

Today My Loss Felt: To Get My Mind Off Of My Loss, I
                                        Did:

I Am Starting To: Today God Comforted Me By:

I'm Really Surprised That I: Helpful Things That Have Been Done
                                        And/Or Said To Help Me Heal:

I Am Releasing

Date: I Am Feeling:

Morning Thoughts

I Want: Today's Declaration:

I Really Miss: I Am Allowing Myself Time To:

I Believe: I Laid Awake/Fell Asleep Last Night
                                         Thinking:

Nightly Thoughts

Today My Loss Felt: To Get My Mind Off Of My Loss, I
                                         Did:

I Am Starting To: Today God Comforted Me By:

I'm Really Surprised That I: Helpful Things That Have Been Done
                                         And/Or Said To Help Me Heal:

I Am Releasing

Date: I Am Feeling:

Morning Thoughts

I Want: Today's Declaration:

I Really Miss: I Am Allowing Myself Time To:

I Believe: I Laid Awake/Fell Asleep Last Night
                                         Thinking:

Nightly Thoughts

Today My Loss Felt: To Get My Mind Off Of My Loss, I
                                         Did:

I Am Starting To: Today God Comforted Me By:

I'm Really Surprised That I: Helpful Things That Have Been Done
                                         And/Or Said To Help Me Heal:

Grieving Thoughts

Because of you, I keep moving forward.

I Am Releasing

Date: I Am Feeling:

Morning Thoughts

I Want: Today's Declaration:

I Really Miss: I Am Allowing Myself Time To:

I Believe: I Laid Awake/Fell Asleep Last Night
                                         Thinking:

Nightly Thoughts

Today My Loss Felt: To Get My Mind Off Of My Loss, I
                                         Did:

I Am Starting To: Today God Comforted Me By:

I'm Really Surprised That I: Helpful Things That Have Been Done
                                         And/Or Said To Help Me Heal:

I Am Releasing

Date: I Am Feeling:

Morning Thoughts

I Want: Today's Declaration:

I Really Miss: I Am Allowing Myself Time To:

I Believe: I Laid Awake/Fell Asleep Last Night
                                          Thinking:

Nightly Thoughts

Today My Loss Felt: To Get My Mind Off Of My Loss, I
                                          Did:

I Am Starting To: Today God Comforted Me By:

I'm Really Surprised That I: Helpful Things That Have Been Done
                                          And/Or Said To Help Me Heal:

I release you unto God.

I felt like you transitioned over....

I Am Releasing

Date: I Am Feeling:

Morning Thoughts

I Want: Today's Declaration:

I Really Miss: I Am Allowing Myself Time To:

I Believe: I Laid Awake/Fell Asleep Last Night
                                               Thinking:

Nightly Thoughts

Today My Loss Felt: To Get My Mind Off Of My Loss, I
                                               Did:

I Am Starting To: Today God Comforted Me By:

I'm Really Surprised That I: Helpful Things That Have Been Done
                                               And/Or Said To Help Me Heal:

I Am Releasing

Date: I Am Feeling:

Morning Thoughts

I Want: Today's Declaration:

I Really Miss: I Am Allowing Myself Time To:

I Believe: I Laid Awake/Fell Asleep Last Night
                                   Thinking:

Nightly Thoughts

Today My Loss Felt: To Get My Mind Off Of My Loss, I
                                   Did:

I Am Starting To: Today God Comforted Me By:

I'm Really Surprised That I: Helpful Things That Have Been Done
                                   And/Or Said To Help Me Heal:

You didn't just tell me, you showed me....

As long as
I'm alive,
you will
forever live.

I forgive you.

I Am Releasing

Date: I Am Feeling:

Morning Thoughts

I Want: Today's Declaration:

I Really Miss: I Am Allowing Myself Time To:

I Believe: I Laid Awake/Fell Asleep Last Night
                                   Thinking:

Nightly Thoughts

Today My Loss Felt: To Get My Mind Off Of My Loss, I
                                   Did:

I Am Starting To: Today God Comforted Me By:

I'm Really Surprised That I: Helpful Things That Have Been Done
                                   And/Or Said To Help Me Heal:

I Am Releasing

Date: I Am Feeling:

Morning Thoughts

I Want: Today's Declaration:

I Really Miss: I Am Allowing Myself Time To:

I Believe: I Laid Awake/Fell Asleep Last Night
                                         Thinking:

Nightly Thoughts

Today My Loss Felt: To Get My Mind Off Of My Loss, I
                                         Did:

I Am Starting To: Today God Comforted Me By:

I'm Really Surprised That I: Helpful Things That Have Been Done
                                         And/Or Said To Help Me Heal:

A letter to the one I've lost....

When I visit your grave I....

I Am Releasing

Date: I Am Feeling:

Morning Thoughts

I Want: Today's Declaration:

I Really Miss: I Am Allowing Myself Time To:

I Believe: I Laid Awake/Fell Asleep Last Night
                                         Thinking:

Nightly Thoughts

Today My Loss Felt: To Get My Mind Off Of My Loss, I
                                         Did:

I Am Starting To: Today God Comforted Me By:

I'm Really Surprised That I: Helpful Things That Have Been Done
                                         And/Or Said To Help Me Heal:

I Am Releasing

Date: I Am Feeling:

Morning Thoughts

I Want: Today's Declaration:

I Really Miss: I Am Allowing Myself Time To:

I Believe: I Laid Awake/Fell Asleep Last Night
                                   Thinking:

Nightly Thoughts

Today My Loss Felt: To Get My Mind Off Of My Loss, I
                                   Did:

I Am Starting To: Today God Comforted Me By:

I'm Really Surprised That I: Helpful Things That Have Been Done
                                   And/Or Said To Help Me Heal:

I Am Releasing

Date: I Am Feeling:

Morning Thoughts

I Want: Today's Declaration:

I Really Miss: I Am Allowing Myself Time To:

I Believe: I Laid Awake/Fell Asleep Last Night
                                   Thinking:

Nightly Thoughts

Today My Loss Felt: To Get My Mind Off Of My Loss, I
                                   Did:

I Am Starting To: Today God Comforted Me By:

I'm Really Surprised That I: Helpful Things That Have Been Done
                                   And/Or Said To Help Me Heal:

Grieving Thoughts

Activities that I partake in that help me to heal from this pain of losing you....

I Am Releasing

Date: I Am Feeling:

Morning Thoughts

I Want: Today's Declaration:

I Really Miss: I Am Allowing Myself Time To:

I Believe: I Laid Awake/Fell Asleep Last Night
                                         Thinking:

Nightly Thoughts

Today My Loss Felt: To Get My Mind Off Of My Loss, I
                                         Did:

I Am Starting To: Today God Comforted Me By:

I'm Really Surprised That I: Helpful Things That Have Been Done
                                         And/Or Said To Help Me Heal:

I Am Releasing

Date: I Am Feeling:

Morning Thoughts

I Want: Today's Declaration:

I Really Miss: I Am Allowing Myself Time To:

I Believe: I Laid Awake/Fell Asleep Last Night
                                         Thinking:

Nightly Thoughts

Today My Loss Felt: To Get My Mind Off Of My Loss, I
                                         Did:

I Am Starting To: Today God Comforted Me By:

I'm Really Surprised That I: Helpful Things That Have Been Done
                                         And/Or Said To Help Me Heal:

I Am Releasing

Date: I Am Feeling:

Morning Thoughts

I Want: Today's Declaration:

I Really Miss: I Am Allowing Myself Time To:

I Believe: I Laid Awake/Fell Asleep Last Night
                                         Thinking:

Nightly Thoughts

Today My Loss Felt: To Get My Mind Off Of My Loss, I
                                         Did:

I Am Starting To: Today God Comforted Me By:

I'm Really Surprised That I: Helpful Things That Have Been Done
                                         And/Or Said To Help Me Heal:

I Am Releasing

Date: I Am Feeling:

Morning Thoughts

I Want: Today's Declaration:

I Really Miss: I Am Allowing Myself Time To:

I Believe: I Laid Awake/Fell Asleep Last Night
                                         Thinking:

Nightly Thoughts

Today My Loss Felt: To Get My Mind Off Of My Loss, I
                                         Did:

I Am Starting To: Today God Comforted Me By:

I'm Really Surprised That I: Helpful Things That Have Been Done
                                         And/Or Said To Help Me Heal:

Grieving Thoughts

This isn't the end for us.

I Am Releasing

Date: I Am Feeling:

Morning Thoughts

I Want: Today's Declaration:

I Really Miss: I Am Allowing Myself Time To:

I Believe: I Laid Awake/Fell Asleep Last Night
                                         Thinking:

Nightly Thoughts

Today My Loss Felt: To Get My Mind Off Of My Loss, I
                                         Did:

I Am Starting To: Today God Comforted Me By:

I'm Really Surprised That I: Helpful Things That Have Been Done
                                         And/Or Said To Help Me Heal:

I Am Releasing

Date: I Am Feeling:

Morning Thoughts

I Want: Today's Declaration:

I Really Miss: I Am Allowing Myself Time To:

I Believe: I Laid Awake/Fell Asleep Last Night
                                         Thinking:

Nightly Thoughts

Today My Loss Felt: To Get My Mind Off Of My Loss, I
                                         Did:

I Am Starting To: Today God Comforted Me By:

I'm Really Surprised That I: Helpful Things That Have Been Done
                                         And/Or Said To Help Me Heal:

I Am Releasing

Date: I Am Feeling:

Morning Thoughts

I Want: Today's Declaration:

I Really Miss: I Am Allowing Myself Time To:

I Believe: I Laid Awake/Fell Asleep Last Night
                                         Thinking:

Nightly Thoughts

Today My Loss Felt: To Get My Mind Off Of My Loss, I
                                         Did:

I Am Starting To: Today God Comforted Me By:

I'm Really Surprised That I: Helpful Things That Have Been Done
                                         And/Or Said To Help Me Heal:

After you transitioned over, I....

My list of things unsaid....

I Am Releasing

Date: I Am Feeling:

Morning Thoughts

I Want: Today's Declaration:

I Really Miss: I Am Allowing Myself Time To:

I Believe: I Laid Awake/Fell Asleep Last Night
                                                Thinking:

Nightly Thoughts

Today My Loss Felt: To Get My Mind Off Of My Loss, I
                                                Did:

I Am Starting To: Today God Comforted Me By:

I'm Really Surprised That I: Helpful Things That Have Been Done
                                                And/Or Said To Help Me Heal:

I Am Releasing

Date: I Am Feeling:

Morning Thoughts

I Want: Today's Declaration:

I Really Miss: I Am Allowing Myself Time To:

I Believe: I Laid Awake/Fell Asleep Last Night
                                         Thinking:

Nightly Thoughts

Today My Loss Felt: To Get My Mind Off Of My Loss, I
                                         Did:

I Am Starting To: Today God Comforted Me By:

I'm Really Surprised That I: Helpful Things That Have Been Done
                                         And/Or Said To Help Me Heal:

I Am Releasing

Date: I Am Feeling:

Morning Thoughts

I Want: Today's Declaration:

I Really Miss: I Am Allowing Myself Time To:

I Believe: I Laid Awake/Fell Asleep Last Night
                                         Thinking:

Nightly Thoughts

Today My Loss Felt: To Get My Mind Off Of My Loss, I
                                         Did:

I Am Starting To: Today God Comforted Me By:

I'm Really Surprised That I: Helpful Things That Have Been Done
                                         And/Or Said To Help Me Heal:

I Am Releasing

Date: I Am Feeling:

Morning Thoughts

I Want: Today's Declaration:

I Really Miss: I Am Allowing Myself Time To:

I Believe: I Laid Awake/Fell Asleep Last Night
                                         Thinking:

Nightly Thoughts

Today My Loss Felt: To Get My Mind Off Of My Loss, I
                                         Did:

I Am Starting To: Today God Comforted Me By:

I'm Really Surprised That I: Helpful Things That Have Been Done
                                         And/Or Said To Help Me Heal:

I Am Releasing

Date: I Am Feeling:

Morning Thoughts

I Want: Today's Declaration:

I Really Miss: I Am Allowing Myself Time To:

I Believe: I Laid Awake/Fell Asleep Last Night
                                          Thinking:

Nightly Thoughts

Today My Loss Felt: To Get My Mind Off Of My Loss, I
                                          Did:

I Am Starting To: Today God Comforted Me By:

I'm Really Surprised That I: Helpful Things That Have Been Done
                                          And/Or Said To Help Me Heal:

Grieving Thoughts

Closure for me looks and feels like....

I Am Releasing

Date: I Am Feeling:

Morning Thoughts

I Want: Today's Declaration:

I Really Miss: I Am Allowing Myself Time To:

I Believe: I Laid Awake/Fell Asleep Last Night
                                         Thinking:

Nightly Thoughts

Today My Loss Felt: To Get My Mind Off Of My Loss, I
                                         Did:

I Am Starting To: Today God Comforted Me By:

I'm Really Surprised That I: Helpful Things That Have Been Done
                                         And/Or Said To Help Me Heal:

Grieving Thoughts

THE NEXT 60 DAYS:

I Am Coping

I Am Coping

Date: Today's Scripture Of Study:

Morning Thoughts

Today I Choose To Focus On: I Know:

Today I Choose To Celebrate You By   I Am At Peace Knowing:
Remembering:

                                         Today I Am Taking These Steps To
I Am Leaning On: Move Forward (List Them):

Nightly Thoughts

Today I Was Really Feeling: Today I Talked More About:

God Has Shown Me: Today I Lived In The Moment By:

I Thought I Couldn't Go On But I   I Know That You Are:
Know I:

I Am Coping

Date: Today's Scripture Of Study:

Morning Thoughts

Today I Choose To Focus On: I Know:

Today I Choose To Celebrate You By Remembering: I Am At Peace Knowing:

I Am Leaning On: Today I Am Taking These Steps To Move Forward (List Them):

Nightly Thoughts

Today I Was Really Feeling: Today I Talked More About:

God Has Shown Me: Today I Lived In The Moment By:

I Thought I Couldn't Go On But I Know I: I Know That You Are:

The story of your life in my words....

I Am Coping

Date: _____   Today's Scripture Of Study: _____

Morning Thoughts

Today I Choose To Focus On: I Know:

Today I Choose To Celebrate You By   I Am At Peace Knowing:
Remembering:

                                     Today I Am Taking These Steps To
I Am Leaning On: Move Forward (List Them):

Nightly Thoughts

Today I Was Really Feeling: Today I Talked More About:

God Has Shown Me: Today I Lived In The Moment By:

I Thought I Couldn't Go On But I   I Know That You Are:
Know I:

I Am Coping

Date: Today's Scripture Of Study:

Morning Thoughts

Today I Choose To Focus On:

I Know:

Today I Choose To Celebrate You By Remembering:

I Am At Peace Knowing:

I Am Leaning On:

Today I Am Taking These Steps To Move Forward (List Them):

Nightly Thoughts

Today I Was Really Feeling:

Today I Talked More About:

God Has Shown Me:

Today I Lived In The Moment By:

I Thought I Couldn't Go On But I Know I:

I Know That You Are:

I Am Coping

Date: Today's Scripture Of Study:

Morning Thoughts

Today I Choose To Focus On: I Know:

Today I Choose To Celebrate You By   I Am At Peace Knowing:
Remembering:

                                         Today I Am Taking These Steps To
I Am Leaning On: Move Forward (List Them):

Nightly Thoughts

Today I Was Really Feeling: Today I Talked More About:

God Has Shown Me: Today I Lived In The Moment By:

I Thought I Couldn't Go On But I   I Know That You Are:
Know I:

I Am Coping

Date: Today's Scripture Of Study:

Morning Thoughts

Today I Choose To Focus On: I Know:

Today I Choose To Celebrate You By   I Am At Peace Knowing:
Remembering:

                                        Today I Am Taking These Steps To
I Am Leaning On: Move Forward (List Them):

Nightly Thoughts

Today I Was Really Feeling: Today I Talked More About:

God Has Shown Me: Today I Lived In The Moment By:

I Thought I Couldn't Go On But I   I Know That You Are:
Know I:

Ten things we shared in common....

I understand that God wanted you home.

You gave me so much to remember.

I Am Coping

Date: Today's Scripture Of Study:

Morning Thoughts

Today I Choose To Focus On: I Know:

Today I Choose To Celebrate You By   I Am At Peace Knowing:
Remembering:

                                       Today I Am Taking These Steps To
I Am Leaning On: Move Forward (List Them):

Nightly Thoughts

Today I Was Really Feeling: Today I Talked More About:

God Has Shown Me: Today I Lived In The Moment By:

I Thought I Couldn't Go On But I   I Know That You Are:
Know I:

I Am Coping

Date: _____   Today's Scripture Of Study: _____

Morning Thoughts

Today I Choose To Focus On: I Know:

Today I Choose To Celebrate You By   I Am At Peace Knowing:
Remembering:

                                               Today I Am Taking These Steps To
I Am Leaning On: Move Forward (List Them):

Nightly Thoughts

Today I Was Really Feeling: Today I Talked More About:

God Has Shown Me: Today I Lived In The Moment By:

I Thought I Couldn't Go On But I   I Know That You Are:
Know I:

Coping And Moving Forward Thoughts

I Am Coping

Date: Today's Scripture Of Study:

Morning Thoughts

Today I Choose To Focus On: I Know:

Today I Choose To Celebrate You By   I Am At Peace Knowing:
Remembering:

                                     Today I Am Taking These Steps To
I Am Leaning On: Move Forward (List Them):

Nightly Thoughts

Today I Was Really Feeling: Today I Talked More About:

God Has Shown Me: Today I Lived In The Moment By:

I Thought I Couldn't Go On But I   I Know That You Are:
Know I:

I Am Coping

Date: Today's Scripture Of Study:

Morning Thoughts

Today I Choose To Focus On: I Know:

Today I Choose To Celebrate You By   I Am At Peace Knowing:
Remembering:

                                         Today I Am Taking These Steps To
I Am Leaning On: Move Forward (List Them):

Nightly Thoughts

Today I Was Really Feeling: Today I Talked More About:

God Has Shown Me: Today I Lived In The Moment By:

I Thought I Couldn't Go On But I   I Know That You Are:
Know I:

I miss....

What we had that was special....

I Am Coping

Date: Today's Scripture Of Study:

Morning Thoughts

Today I Choose To Focus On:

I Know:

Today I Choose To Celebrate You By Remembering:

I Am At Peace Knowing:

I Am Leaning On:

Today I Am Taking These Steps To Move Forward (List Them):

Nightly Thoughts

Today I Was Really Feeling:

Today I Talked More About:

God Has Shown Me:

Today I Lived In The Moment By:

I Thought I Couldn't Go On But I Know I:

I Know That You Are:

I Am Coping

Date: Today's Scripture Of Study:

Morning Thoughts

Today I Choose To Focus On:

I Know:

Today I Choose To Celebrate You By Remembering:

I Am At Peace Knowing:

I Am Leaning On:

Today I Am Taking These Steps To Move Forward (List Them):

Nightly Thoughts

Today I Was Really Feeling:

Today I Talked More About:

God Has Shown Me:

Today I Lived In The Moment By:

I Thought I Couldn't Go On But I Know I:

I Know That You Are:

I just
love you.

I Am Coping

Date: _____   Today's Scripture Of Study: _____

Morning Thoughts

Today I Choose To Focus On:

I Know:

Today I Choose To Celebrate You By Remembering:

I Am At Peace Knowing:

I Am Leaning On:

Today I Am Taking These Steps To Move Forward (List Them):

Nightly Thoughts

Today I Was Really Feeling:

Today I Talked More About:

God Has Shown Me:

Today I Lived In The Moment By:

I Thought I Couldn't Go On But I Know I:

I Know That You Are:

I Am Coping

Date: _____   Today's Scripture Of Study: _____

Morning Thoughts

Today I Choose To Focus On:

I Know:

Today I Choose To Celebrate You By Remembering:

I Am At Peace Knowing:

I Am Leaning On:

Today I Am Taking These Steps To Move Forward (List Them):

Nightly Thoughts

Today I Was Really Feeling:

Today I Talked More About:

God Has Shown Me:

Today I Lived In The Moment By:

I Thought I Couldn't Go On But I Know I:

I Know That You Are:

I Am Coping

Date: Today's Scripture Of Study:

Morning Thoughts

Today I Choose To Focus On: | I Know:

Today I Choose To Celebrate You By | I Am At Peace Knowing:
Remembering:

                                     | Today I Am Taking These Steps To
I Am Leaning On: | Move Forward (List Them):

Nightly Thoughts

Today I Was Really Feeling: | Today I Talked More About:

God Has Shown Me: | Today I Lived In The Moment By:

I Thought I Couldn't Go On But I | I Know That You Are:
Know I:

We'll always share so much.

I Am Coping

Date: Today's Scripture Of Study:

Morning Thoughts

Today I Choose To Focus On: I Know:

Today I Choose To Celebrate You By   I Am At Peace Knowing:
Remembering:

I Am Leaning On: Today I Am Taking These Steps To
                                      Move Forward (List Them):

Nightly Thoughts

Today I Was Really Feeling: Today I Talked More About:

God Has Shown Me: Today I Lived In The Moment By:

I Thought I Couldn't Go On But I   I Know That You Are:
Know I:

I Am Coping

Date: Today's Scripture Of Study:

Morning Thoughts

Today I Choose To Focus On: I Know:

Today I Choose To Celebrate You By   I Am At Peace Knowing:
Remembering:

                                         Today I Am Taking These Steps To
I Am Leaning On: Move Forward (List Them):

Nightly Thoughts

Today I Was Really Feeling: Today I Talked More About:

God Has Shown Me: Today I Lived In The Moment By:

I Thought I Couldn't Go On But I   I Know That You Are:
Know I:

110

Coping And Moving Forward Thoughts

I Am Coping

Date: Today's Scripture Of Study:

Morning Thoughts

Today I Choose To Focus On:

I Know:

Today I Choose To Celebrate You By Remembering:

I Am At Peace Knowing:

I Am Leaning On:

Today I Am Taking These Steps To Move Forward (List Them):

Nightly Thoughts

Today I Was Really Feeling:

Today I Talked More About:

God Has Shown Me:

Today I Lived In The Moment By:

I Thought I Couldn't Go On But I Know I:

I Know That You Are:

I Am Coping

Date: Today's Scripture Of Study:

Morning Thoughts

Today I Choose To Focus On: I Know:

Today I Choose To Celebrate You By   I Am At Peace Knowing:
Remembering:

                                      Today I Am Taking These Steps To
I Am Leaning On: Move Forward (List Them):

Nightly Thoughts

Today I Was Really Feeling: Today I Talked More About:

God Has Shown Me: Today I Lived In The Moment By:

I Thought I Couldn't Go On But I   I Know That You Are:
Know I:

When I tell people about you, I tell them....

I move forward taking you with me.

I Am Coping

Date: _____   Today's Scripture Of Study: _____

Morning Thoughts

Today I Choose To Focus On: I Know:

Today I Choose To Celebrate You By   I Am At Peace Knowing:
Remembering:

                                    Today I Am Taking These Steps To
I Am Leaning On: Move Forward (List Them):

Nightly Thoughts

Today I Was Really Feeling: Today I Talked More About:

God Has Shown Me: Today I Lived In The Moment By:

I Thought I Couldn't Go On But I   I Know That You Are:
Know I:

I Am Coping

Date: Today's Scripture Of Study:

Morning Thoughts

Today I Choose To Focus On:

I Know:

Today I Choose To Celebrate You By Remembering:

I Am At Peace Knowing:

I Am Leaning On:

Today I Am Taking These Steps To Move Forward (List Them):

Nightly Thoughts

Today I Was Really Feeling:

Today I Talked More About:

God Has Shown Me:

Today I Lived In The Moment By:

I Thought I Couldn't Go On But I Know I:

I Know That You Are:

I Am Coping

Date: _____   Today's Scripture Of Study: _____

Morning Thoughts

Today I Choose To Focus On: I Know:

Today I Choose To Celebrate You By   I Am At Peace Knowing:
Remembering:

                                             Today I Am Taking These Steps To
I Am Leaning On: Move Forward (List Them):

Nightly Thoughts

Today I Was Really Feeling: Today I Talked More About:

God Has Shown Me: Today I Lived In The Moment By:

I Thought I Couldn't Go On But I   I Know That You Are:
Know I:

Coping And Moving Forward Thoughts

I Am Coping

Date: _____   Today's Scripture Of Study: _____

Morning Thoughts

Today I Choose To Focus On: I Know:

Today I Choose To Celebrate You By   I Am At Peace Knowing:
Remembering:

                                         Today I Am Taking These Steps To
                                         Move Forward (List Them):
I Am Leaning On:

Nightly Thoughts

Today I Was Really Feeling: Today I Talked More About:

God Has Shown Me: Today I Lived In The Moment By:

I Thought I Couldn't Go On But I   I Know That You Are:
Know I:

I Am Coping

Date: Today's Scripture Of Study:

Morning Thoughts

Today I Choose To Focus On: I Know:

Today I Choose To Celebrate You By   I Am At Peace Knowing:
Remembering:

                                       Today I Am Taking These Steps To
I Am Leaning On: Move Forward (List Them):

Nightly Thoughts

Today I Was Really Feeling: Today I Talked More About:

God Has Shown Me: Today I Lived In The Moment By:

I Thought I Couldn't Go On But I   I Know That You Are:
Know I:

The type of support that I need right now....

I become vulnerable when I talk about....

I Am Coping

Date: Today's Scripture Of Study:

Morning Thoughts

Today I Choose To Focus On: I Know:

Today I Choose To Celebrate You By   I Am At Peace Knowing:
Remembering:

                                         Today I Am Taking These Steps To
I Am Leaning On: Move Forward (List Them):

Nightly Thoughts

Today I Was Really Feeling: Today I Talked More About:

God Has Shown Me: Today I Lived In The Moment By:

I Thought I Couldn't Go On But I   I Know That You Are:
Know I:

I Am Coping

Date: _____   Today's Scripture Of Study: _____

Morning Thoughts

Today I Choose To Focus On:

I Know:

Today I Choose To Celebrate You By Remembering:

I Am At Peace Knowing:

I Am Leaning On:

Today I Am Taking These Steps To Move Forward (List Them):

Nightly Thoughts

Today I Was Really Feeling:

Today I Talked More About:

God Has Shown Me:

Today I Lived In The Moment By:

I Thought I Couldn't Go On But I Know I:

I Know That You Are:

Coping And Moving Forward Thoughts

I Am Coping

Date:

Today's Scripture Of Study:

Morning Thoughts

Today I Choose To Focus On:

I Know:

Today I Choose To Celebrate You By Remembering:

I Am At Peace Knowing:

I Am Leaning On:

Today I Am Taking These Steps To Move Forward (List Them):

Nightly Thoughts

Today I Was Really Feeling:

Today I Talked More About:

God Has Shown Me:

Today I Lived In The Moment By:

I Thought I Couldn't Go On But I Know I:

I Know That You Are:

I Am Coping

Date: Today's Scripture Of Study:

Morning Thoughts

Today I Choose To Focus On: I Know:

Today I Choose To Celebrate You By   I Am At Peace Knowing:
Remembering:

                                         Today I Am Taking These Steps To
I Am Leaning On: Move Forward (List Them):

Nightly Thoughts

Today I Was Really Feeling: Today I Talked More About:

God Has Shown Me: Today I Lived In The Moment By:

I Thought I Couldn't Go On But I   I Know That You Are:
Know I:

I smile knowing....

I can now fight through....

I Am Coping

Date: Today's Scripture Of Study:

Morning Thoughts

Today I Choose To Focus On: I Know:

Today I Choose To Celebrate You By   I Am At Peace Knowing:
Remembering:

                                         Today I Am Taking These Steps To
I Am Leaning On: Move Forward (List Them):

Nightly Thoughts

Today I Was Really Feeling: Today I Talked More About:

God Has Shown Me: Today I Lived In The Moment By:

I Thought I Couldn't Go On But I   I Know That You Are:
Know I:

I Am Coping

Date: _____   Today's Scripture Of Study: _____

Morning Thoughts

Today I Choose To Focus On: I Know:

Today I Choose To Celebrate You By   I Am At Peace Knowing:
Remembering:

                                          Today I Am Taking These Steps To
I Am Leaning On: Move Forward (List Them):

Nightly Thoughts

Today I Was Really Feeling: Today I Talked More About:

God Has Shown Me: Today I Lived In The Moment By:

I Thought I Couldn't Go On But I   I Know That You Are:
Know I:

I Am Coping

Date: Today's Scripture Of Study:

Morning Thoughts

Today I Choose To Focus On: | I Know:

Today I Choose To Celebrate You By Remembering: | I Am At Peace Knowing:

I Am Leaning On: | Today I Am Taking These Steps To Move Forward (List Them):

Nightly Thoughts

Today I Was Really Feeling: | Today I Talked More About:

God Has Shown Me: | Today I Lived In The Moment By:

I Thought I Couldn't Go On But I Know I: | I Know That You Are:

Because of you....

I Am Coping

Date: Today's Scripture Of Study:

Morning Thoughts

Today I Choose To Focus On: I Know:

Today I Choose To Celebrate You By   I Am At Peace Knowing:
Remembering:

                                         Today I Am Taking These Steps To
I Am Leaning On: Move Forward (List Them):

Nightly Thoughts

Today I Was Really Feeling: Today I Talked More About:

God Has Shown Me: Today I Lived In The Moment By:

I Thought I Couldn't Go On But I   I Know That You Are:
Know I:

I Am Coping

Date: _____   Today's Scripture Of Study: _____

Morning Thoughts

Today I Choose To Focus On: I Know:

Today I Choose To Celebrate You By   I Am At Peace Knowing:
Remembering:

I Am Leaning On: Today I Am Taking These Steps To
Move Forward (List Them):

Nightly Thoughts

Today I Was Really Feeling: Today I Talked More About:

God Has Shown Me: Today I Lived In The Moment By:

I Thought I Couldn't Go On But I   I Know That You Are:
Know I:

I Am Coping

Date: _____   Today's Scripture Of Study: _____

Morning Thoughts

Today I Choose To Focus On:

I Know:

Today I Choose To Celebrate You By Remembering:

I Am At Peace Knowing:

I Am Leaning On:

Today I Am Taking These Steps To Move Forward (List Them):

Nightly Thoughts

Today I Was Really Feeling:

Today I Talked More About:

God Has Shown Me:

Today I Lived In The Moment By:

I Thought I Couldn't Go On But I Know I:

I Know That You Are:

I Am Coping

Date: Today's Scripture Of Study:

Morning Thoughts

Today I Choose To Focus On: I Know:

Today I Choose To Celebrate You By   I Am At Peace Knowing:
Remembering:

I Am Leaning On: Today I Am Taking These Steps To
                                         Move Forward (List Them):

Nightly Thoughts

Today I Was Really Feeling: Today I Talked More About:

God Has Shown Me: Today I Lived In The Moment By:

I Thought I Couldn't Go On But I   I Know That You Are:
Know I:

Thank you
for allowing
me to be a
part of
your life.

I will continue your legacy.

I know you are rooting for me.

I Am Coping

Date: Today's Scripture Of Study:

Morning Thoughts

Today I Choose To Focus On: I Know:

Today I Choose To Celebrate You By   I Am At Peace Knowing:
Remembering:

                                     Today I Am Taking These Steps To
                                     Move Forward (List Them):
I Am Leaning On:

Nightly Thoughts

Today I Was Really Feeling: Today I Talked More About:

God Has Shown Me: Today I Lived In The Moment By:

I Thought I Couldn't Go On But I   I Know That You Are:
Know I:

I Am Coping

Date: Today's Scripture Of Study:

Morning Thoughts

Today I Choose To Focus On: I Know:

Today I Choose To Celebrate You By   I Am At Peace Knowing:
Remembering:

                                         Today I Am Taking These Steps To
I Am Leaning On: Move Forward (List Them):

Nightly Thoughts

Today I Was Really Feeling: Today I Talked More About:

God Has Shown Me: Today I Lived In The Moment By:

I Thought I Couldn't Go On But I   I Know That You Are:
Know I:

I Am Coping

Date: _____   Today's Scripture Of Study: _____

Morning Thoughts

Today I Choose To Focus On: I Know:

Today I Choose To Celebrate You By   I Am At Peace Knowing:
Remembering:

Today I Am Taking These Steps To
Move Forward (List Them):

I Am Leaning On:

Nightly Thoughts

Today I Was Really Feeling: Today I Talked More About:

God Has Shown Me: Today I Lived In The Moment By:

I Thought I Couldn't Go On But I   I Know That You Are:
Know I:

I Am Coping

Date: _____   Today's Scripture Of Study: _____

Morning Thoughts

Today I Choose To Focus On:

I Know:

Today I Choose To Celebrate You By Remembering:

I Am At Peace Knowing:

I Am Leaning On:

Today I Am Taking These Steps To Move Forward (List Them):

Nightly Thoughts

Today I Was Really Feeling:

Today I Talked More About:

God Has Shown Me:

Today I Lived In The Moment By:

I Thought I Couldn't Go On But I Know I:

I Know That You Are:

Five things you have taught me....

Jesus said to her, "I am the resurrection and the life. The one who believes in me will live, even though they die; and whoever lives by believing in me will never die. Do you believe this?"

— John 11:25-26

I Am Coping

Date: _____   Today's Scripture Of Study: _____

Morning Thoughts

Today I Choose To Focus On:

I Know:

Today I Choose To Celebrate You By Remembering:

I Am At Peace Knowing:

I Am Leaning On:

Today I Am Taking These Steps To Move Forward (List Them):

Nightly Thoughts

Today I Was Really Feeling:

Today I Talked More About:

God Has Shown Me:

Today I Lived In The Moment By:

I Thought I Couldn't Go On But I Know I:

I Know That You Are:

I Am Coping

Date:

Today's Scripture Of Study:

Morning Thoughts

Today I Choose To Focus On:

I Know:

Today I Choose To Celebrate You By Remembering:

I Am At Peace Knowing:

I Am Leaning On:

Today I Am Taking These Steps To Move Forward (List Them):

Nightly Thoughts

Today I Was Really Feeling:

Today I Talked More About:

God Has Shown Me:

Today I Lived In The Moment By:

I Thought I Couldn't Go On But I Know I:

I Know That You Are:

Coping And Moving Forward Thoughts

I Am Coping

Date: _____   Today's Scripture Of Study: _____

Morning Thoughts

Today I Choose To Focus On: I Know:

Today I Choose To Celebrate You By   I Am At Peace Knowing:
Remembering:

                                         Today I Am Taking These Steps To
I Am Leaning On: Move Forward (List Them):

Nightly Thoughts

Today I Was Really Feeling: Today I Talked More About:

God Has Shown Me: Today I Lived In The Moment By:

I Thought I Couldn't Go On But I   I Know That You Are:
Know I:

I Am Coping

Date: Today's Scripture Of Study:

Morning Thoughts

Today I Choose To Focus On: I Know:

Today I Choose To Celebrate You By   I Am At Peace Knowing:
Remembering:

                                         Today I Am Taking These Steps To
I Am Leaning On: Move Forward (List Them):

Nightly Thoughts

Today I Was Really Feeling: Today I Talked More About:

God Has Shown Me: Today I Lived In The Moment By:

I Thought I Couldn't Go On But I   I Know That You Are:
Know I:

I Am Coping

Date: Today's Scripture Of Study:

Morning Thoughts

Today I Choose To Focus On: I Know:

Today I Choose To Celebrate You By   I Am At Peace Knowing:
Remembering:

                                         Today I Am Taking These Steps To
I Am Leaning On: Move Forward (List Them):

Nightly Thoughts

Today I Was Really Feeling: Today I Talked More About:

God Has Shown Me: Today I Lived In The Moment By:

I Thought I Couldn't Go On But I   I Know That You Are:
Know I:

I will always feel you.

I will never say
goodbye.
I will just say
see you later.

I Am Coping

Date: Today's Scripture Of Study:

Morning Thoughts

Today I Choose To Focus On: I Know:

Today I Choose To Celebrate You By   I Am At Peace Knowing:
Remembering:

                                         Today I Am Taking These Steps To
                                         Move Forward (List Them):
I Am Leaning On:

Nightly Thoughts

Today I Was Really Feeling: Today I Talked More About:

God Has Shown Me: Today I Lived In The Moment By:

I Thought I Couldn't Go On But I   I Know That You Are:
Know I:

I Am Coping

Date: Today's Scripture Of Study:

Morning Thoughts

Today I Choose To Focus On: I Know:

Today I Choose To Celebrate You By   I Am At Peace Knowing:
Remembering:

                                       Today I Am Taking These Steps To
I Am Leaning On: Move Forward (List Them):

Nightly Thoughts

Today I Was Really Feeling: Today I Talked More About:

God Has Shown Me: Today I Lived In The Moment By:

I Thought I Couldn't Go On But I   I Know That You Are:
Know I:

"Blessed are those who mourn, for they will be comforted." — Matthew 5:4

You left behind....

I Am Coping

Date:

Today's Scripture Of Study:

Morning Thoughts

Today I Choose To Focus On:

I Know:

Today I Choose To Celebrate You By Remembering:

I Am At Peace Knowing:

I Am Leaning On:

Today I Am Taking These Steps To Move Forward (List Them):

Nightly Thoughts

Today I Was Really Feeling:

Today I Talked More About:

God Has Shown Me:

Today I Lived In The Moment By:

I Thought I Couldn't Go On But I Know I:

I Know That You Are:

I Am Coping

Date: Today's Scripture Of Study:

Morning Thoughts

Today I Choose To Focus On: I Know:

Today I Choose To Celebrate You By   I Am At Peace Knowing:
Remembering:

                                         Today I Am Taking These Steps To
I Am Leaning On: Move Forward (List Them):

Nightly Thoughts

Today I Was Really Feeling: Today I Talked More About:

God Has Shown Me: Today I Lived In The Moment By:

I Thought I Couldn't Go On But I   I Know That You Are:
Know I:

I Am Coping

Date: Today's Scripture Of Study:

Morning Thoughts

Today I Choose To Focus On: I Know:

Today I Choose To Celebrate You By   I Am At Peace Knowing:
Remembering:

                                     Today I Am Taking These Steps To
I Am Leaning On: Move Forward (List Them):

Nightly Thoughts

Today I Was Really Feeling: Today I Talked More About:

God Has Shown Me: Today I Lived In The Moment By:

I Thought I Couldn't Go On But I   I Know That You Are:
Know I:

I can move forward happily knowing that you....

It's okay.
I know
you're now
in peace.

I Am Coping

Date: _____   Today's Scripture Of Study: _____

Morning Thoughts

Today I Choose To Focus On:

I Know:

Today I Choose To Celebrate You By Remembering:

I Am At Peace Knowing:

I Am Leaning On:

Today I Am Taking These Steps To Move Forward (List Them):

Nightly Thoughts

Today I Was Really Feeling:

Today I Talked More About:

God Has Shown Me:

Today I Lived In The Moment By:

I Thought I Couldn't Go On But I Know I:

I Know That You Are:

I Am Coping

Date:

Today's Scripture Of Study:

Morning Thoughts

Today I Choose To Focus On:

I Know:

Today I Choose To Celebrate You By Remembering:

I Am At Peace Knowing:

I Am Leaning On:

Today I Am Taking These Steps To Move Forward (List Them):

Nightly Thoughts

Today I Was Really Feeling:

Today I Talked More About:

God Has Shown Me:

Today I Lived In The Moment By:

I Thought I Couldn't Go On But I Know I:

I Know That You Are:

I Am Coping

Date: Today's Scripture Of Study:

Morning Thoughts

Today I Choose To Focus On:

I Know:

Today I Choose To Celebrate You By Remembering:

I Am At Peace Knowing:

I Am Leaning On:

Today I Am Taking These Steps To Move Forward (List Them):

Nightly Thoughts

Today I Was Really Feeling:

Today I Talked More About:

God Has Shown Me:

Today I Lived In The Moment By:

I Thought I Couldn't Go On But I Know I:

I Know That You Are:

I know you want to see me....

I want you to know that I am going to....

I Am Coping

Date: Today's Scripture Of Study:

Morning Thoughts

Today I Choose To Focus On: | I Know:

Today I Choose To Celebrate You By | I Am At Peace Knowing:
Remembering:

I Am Leaning On: | Today I Am Taking These Steps To
                                         | Move Forward (List Them):

Nightly Thoughts

Today I Was Really Feeling: | Today I Talked More About:

God Has Shown Me: | Today I Lived In The Moment By:

I Thought I Couldn't Go On But I | I Know That You Are:
Know I:

I Am Coping

Date: Today's Scripture Of Study:

Morning Thoughts

Today I Choose To Focus On: I Know:

Today I Choose To Celebrate You By   I Am At Peace Knowing:
Remembering:

                                     Today I Am Taking These Steps To
I Am Leaning On: Move Forward (List Them):

Nightly Thoughts

Today I Was Really Feeling: Today I Talked More About:

God Has Shown Me: Today I Lived In The Moment By:

I Thought I Couldn't Go On But I   I Know That You Are:
Know I:

I Am Coping

Date: _____ Today's Scripture Of Study: _____

Morning Thoughts

Today I Choose To Focus On:

I Know:

Today I Choose To Celebrate You By Remembering:

I Am At Peace Knowing:

I Am Leaning On:

Today I Am Taking These Steps To Move Forward (List Them):

Nightly Thoughts

Today I Was Really Feeling:

Today I Talked More About:

God Has Shown Me:

Today I Lived In The Moment By:

I Thought I Couldn't Go On But I Know I:

I Know That You Are:

Coping And Moving Forward Thoughts

I consider you to be....

I Am Coping

Date: Today's Scripture Of Study:

Morning Thoughts

Today I Choose To Focus On: I Know:

Today I Choose To Celebrate You By   I Am At Peace Knowing:
Remembering:

                                           Today I Am Taking These Steps To
I Am Leaning On: Move Forward (List Them):

Nightly Thoughts

Today I Was Really Feeling: Today I Talked More About:

God Has Shown Me: Today I Lived In The Moment By:

I Thought I Couldn't Go On But I   I Know That You Are:
Know I:

I Am Coping

Date: Today's Scripture Of Study:

Morning Thoughts

Today I Choose To Focus On: I Know:

Today I Choose To Celebrate You By   I Am At Peace Knowing:
Remembering:

                                               Today I Am Taking These Steps To
I Am Leaning On: Move Forward (List Them):

Nightly Thoughts

Today I Was Really Feeling: Today I Talked More About:

God Has Shown Me: Today I Lived In The Moment By:

I Thought I Couldn't Go On But I   I Know That You Are:
Know I:

I Am Coping

Date: _____   Today's Scripture Of Study: _____

Morning Thoughts

Today I Choose To Focus On:

I Know:

Today I Choose To Celebrate You By Remembering:

I Am At Peace Knowing:

I Am Leaning On:

Today I Am Taking These Steps To Move Forward (List Them):

Nightly Thoughts

Today I Was Really Feeling:

Today I Talked More About:

God Has Shown Me:

Today I Lived In The Moment By:

I Thought I Couldn't Go On But I Know I:

I Know That You Are:

A prayer for you....

A prayer for my healing heart....

I Am Coping

Date: Today's Scripture Of Study:

Morning Thoughts

Today I Choose To Focus On: I Know:

Today I Choose To Celebrate You By   I Am At Peace Knowing:
Remembering:

                                                   Today I Am Taking These Steps To
I Am Leaning On: Move Forward (List Them):

Nightly Thoughts

Today I Was Really Feeling: Today I Talked More About:

God Has Shown Me: Today I Lived In The Moment By:

I Thought I Couldn't Go On But I   I Know That You Are:
Know I:

I Am Coping

Date: Today's Scripture Of Study:

Morning Thoughts

Today I Choose To Focus On: I Know:

Today I Choose To Celebrate You By   I Am At Peace Knowing:
Remembering:

                                      Today I Am Taking These Steps To
I Am Leaning On: Move Forward (List Them):

Nightly Thoughts

Today I Was Really Feeling: Today I Talked More About:

God Has Shown Me: Today I Lived In The Moment By:

I Thought I Couldn't Go On But I   I Know That You Are:
Know I:

THESE 60 DAYS:

I Am Being Filled

(fill in this section every night)

I Am Being Filled

Date: Today's Affirmation:

I Woke Up Feeling: Everyday I Want To Say To You:

Biblical Scripture That Is Helping Me: Everyday I Say To Myself:

I Feel Better Knowing: I Sense:

Your Life Has Taught Me: I Know Today You Would Have
                                                 Laughed At:

Something Beautiful That I Saw   Today, My Moving Forward Plan
Today That Reminded Me Of You: Consisted Of:

I Am Being Filled

Date:

I Woke Up Feeling:

Biblical Scripture That Is Helping Me:

I Feel Better Knowing:

Your Life Has Taught Me:

Something Beautiful That I Saw
Today That Reminded Me Of You:

Today's Affirmation:

Everyday I Want To Say To You:

Everyday I Say To Myself:

I Sense:

I Know Today You Would Have
Laughed At:

Today, My Moving Forward Plan
Consisted Of:

I Am Being Filled

Date:

I Woke Up Feeling:

Biblical Scripture That Is Helping Me:

I Feel Better Knowing:

Your Life Has Taught Me:

Something Beautiful That I Saw
Today That Reminded Me Of You:

Today's Affirmation:

Everyday I Want To Say To You:

Everyday I Say To Myself:

I Sense:

I Know Today You Would Have
Laughed At:

Today, My Moving Forward Plan
Consisted Of:

Restoration Thoughts

Laugh and dance. That's what I expect you to do now that you're gone.

I know it's better where you are. I know you are okay.

I Am Being Filled

Date:

I Woke Up Feeling:

Biblical Scripture That Is Helping Me:

I Feel Better Knowing:

Your Life Has Taught Me:

Something Beautiful That I Saw
Today That Reminded Me Of You:

Today's Affirmation:

Everyday I Want To Say To You:

Everyday I Say To Myself:

I Sense:

I Know Today You Would Have
Laughed At:

Today, My Moving Forward Plan
Consisted Of:

I Am Being Filled

Date:

I Woke Up Feeling:

Biblical Scripture That Is Helping Me:

I Feel Better Knowing:

Your Life Has Taught Me:

Something Beautiful That I Saw
Today That Reminded Me Of You:

Today's Affirmation:

Everyday I Want To Say To You:

Everyday I Say To Myself:

I Sense:

I Know Today You Would Have
Laughed At:

Today, My Moving Forward Plan
Consisted Of:

I Am Being Filled

Date:

I Woke Up Feeling:

Biblical Scripture That Is Helping Me:

I Feel Better Knowing:

Your Life Has Taught Me:

Something Beautiful That I Saw
Today That Reminded Me Of You:

Today's Affirmation:

Everyday I Want To Say To You:

Everyday I Say To Myself:

I Sense:

I Know Today You Would Have
Laughed At:

Today, My Moving Forward Plan
Consisted Of:

I Am Being Filled

Date:

I Woke Up Feeling:

Biblical Scripture That Is Helping Me:

I Feel Better Knowing:

Your Life Has Taught Me:

Something Beautiful That I Saw
Today That Reminded Me Of You:

Today's Affirmation:

Everyday I Want To Say To You:

Everyday I Say To Myself:

I Sense:

I Know Today You Would Have
Laughed At:

Today, My Moving Forward Plan
Consisted Of:

I know you are expecting me to....

When your birthday comes around, I will choose to....

A letter to another loved one grieving this loss....

I Am Being Filled

Date:

I Woke Up Feeling:

Biblical Scripture That Is Helping Me:

I Feel Better Knowing:

Your Life Has Taught Me:

Something Beautiful That I Saw
Today That Reminded Me Of You:

Today's Affirmation:

Everyday I Want To Say To You:

Everyday I Say To Myself:

I Sense:

I Know Today You Would Have
Laughed At:

Today, My Moving Forward Plan
Consisted Of:

I Am Being Filled

Date:

I Woke Up Feeling:

Biblical Scripture That Is Helping Me:

I Feel Better Knowing:

Your Life Has Taught Me:

Something Beautiful That I Saw
Today That Reminded Me Of You:

Today's Affirmation:

Everyday I Want To Say To You:

Everyday I Say To Myself:

I Sense:

I Know Today You Would Have
Laughed At:

Today, My Moving Forward Plan
Consisted Of:

I Am Being Filled

Date:

I Woke Up Feeling:

Biblical Scripture That Is Helping Me:

I Feel Better Knowing:

Your Life Has Taught Me:

Something Beautiful That I Saw
Today That Reminded Me Of You:

Today's Affirmation:

Everyday I Want To Say To You:

Everyday I Say To Myself:

I Sense:

I Know Today You Would Have
Laughed At:

Today, My Moving Forward Plan
Consisted Of:

Restoration Thoughts

Lately I've been....

I Am Being Filled

Date:

I Woke Up Feeling:

Biblical Scripture That Is Helping Me:

I Feel Better Knowing:

Your Life Has Taught Me:

Something Beautiful That I Saw Today That Reminded Me Of You:

Today's Affirmation:

Everyday I Want To Say To You:

Everyday I Say To Myself:

I Sense:

I Know Today You Would Have Laughed At:

Today, My Moving Forward Plan Consisted Of:

I Am Being Filled

Date:

I Woke Up Feeling:

Biblical Scripture That Is Helping Me:

I Feel Better Knowing:

Your Life Has Taught Me:

Something Beautiful That I Saw Today That Reminded Me Of You:

Today's Affirmation:

Everyday I Want To Say To You:

Everyday I Say To Myself:

I Sense:

I Know Today You Would Have Laughed At:

Today, My Moving Forward Plan Consisted Of:

I am starting to feel....

How fortunate am I to have experienced your love.

I Am Being Filled

Date:

I Woke Up Feeling:

Biblical Scripture That Is Helping Me:

I Feel Better Knowing:

Your Life Has Taught Me:

Something Beautiful That I Saw
Today That Reminded Me Of You:

Today's Affirmation:

Everyday I Want To Say To You:

Everyday I Say To Myself:

I Sense:

I Know Today You Would Have
Laughed At:

Today, My Moving Forward Plan
Consisted Of:

I Am Being Filled

Date:

I Woke Up Feeling:

Biblical Scripture That Is Helping Me:

I Feel Better Knowing:

Your Life Has Taught Me:

Something Beautiful That I Saw
Today That Reminded Me Of You:

Today's Affirmation:

Everyday I Want To Say To You:

Everyday I Say To Myself:

I Sense:

I Know Today You Would Have
Laughed At:

Today, My Moving Forward Plan
Consisted Of:

I Am Being Filled

Date:

I Woke Up Feeling:

Biblical Scripture That Is Helping Me:

I Feel Better Knowing:

Your Life Has Taught Me:

Something Beautiful That I Saw Today That Reminded Me Of You:

Today's Affirmation:

Everyday I Want To Say To You:

Everyday I Say To Myself:

I Sense:

I Know Today You Would Have Laughed At:

Today, My Moving Forward Plan Consisted Of:

I Am Being Filled

Date:

I Woke Up Feeling:

Biblical Scripture That Is Helping Me:

I Feel Better Knowing:

Your Life Has Taught Me:

Something Beautiful That I Saw
Today That Reminded Me Of You:

Today's Affirmation:

Everyday I Want To Say To You:

Everyday I Say To Myself:

I Sense:

I Know Today You Would Have
Laughed At:

Today, My Moving Forward Plan
Consisted Of:

You're no longer in pain, so I will no longer live in pain either.

I
cherish
you.

You will always be a part of me.

I Am Being Filled

Date:

I Woke Up Feeling:

Biblical Scripture That Is Helping Me:

I Feel Better Knowing:

Your Life Has Taught Me:

Something Beautiful That I Saw
Today That Reminded Me Of You:

Today's Affirmation:

Everyday I Want To Say To You:

Everyday I Say To Myself:

I Sense:

I Know Today You Would Have
Laughed At:

Today, My Moving Forward Plan
Consisted Of:

I Am Being Filled

Date:

I Woke Up Feeling:

Biblical Scripture That Is Helping Me:

I Feel Better Knowing:

Your Life Has Taught Me:

Something Beautiful That I Saw
Today That Reminded Me Of You:

Today's Affirmation:

Everyday I Want To Say To You:

Everyday I Say To Myself:

I Sense:

I Know Today You Would Have
Laughed At:

Today, My Moving Forward Plan
Consisted Of:

I Am Being Filled

Date:

I Woke Up Feeling:

Biblical Scripture That Is Helping Me:

I Feel Better Knowing:

Your Life Has Taught Me:

Something Beautiful That I Saw
Today That Reminded Me Of You:

Today's Affirmation:

Everyday I Want To Say To You:

Everyday I Say To Myself:

I Sense:

I Know Today You Would Have
Laughed At:

Today, My Moving Forward Plan
Consisted Of:

Restoration Thoughts

Ten songs that lift up my mood....

I Am Being Filled

Date:

I Woke Up Feeling:

Biblical Scripture That Is Helping Me:

I Feel Better Knowing:

Your Life Has Taught Me:

Something Beautiful That I Saw
Today That Reminded Me Of You:

Today's Affirmation:

Everyday I Want To Say To You:

Everyday I Say To Myself:

I Sense:

I Know Today You Would Have
Laughed At:

Today, My Moving Forward Plan
Consisted Of:

I Am Being Filled

Date:

I Woke Up Feeling:

Biblical Scripture That Is Helping Me:

I Feel Better Knowing:

Your Life Has Taught Me:

Something Beautiful That I Saw
Today That Reminded Me Of You:

Today's Affirmation:

Everyday I Want To Say To You:

Everyday I Say To Myself:

I Sense:

I Know Today You Would Have
Laughed At:

Today, My Moving Forward Plan
Consisted Of:

I Am Being Filled

Date:

I Woke Up Feeling:

Biblical Scripture That Is Helping Me:

I Feel Better Knowing:

Your Life Has Taught Me:

Something Beautiful That I Saw
Today That Reminded Me Of You:

Today's Affirmation:

Everyday I Want To Say To You:

Everyday I Say To Myself:

I Sense:

I Know Today You Would Have
Laughed At:

Today, My Moving Forward Plan
Consisted Of:

While I will never 'get over' you transitioning over, I am learning to adjust knowing that you are watching.

I Am Being Filled

Date:

I Woke Up Feeling:

Biblical Scripture That Is Helping Me:

I Feel Better Knowing:

Your Life Has Taught Me:

Something Beautiful That I Saw
Today That Reminded Me Of You:

Today's Affirmation:

Everyday I Want To Say To You:

Everyday I Say To Myself:

I Sense:

I Know Today You Would Have
Laughed At:

Today, My Moving Forward Plan
Consisted Of:

I Am Being Filled

Date:

I Woke Up Feeling:

Biblical Scripture That Is Helping Me:

I Feel Better Knowing:

Your Life Has Taught Me:

Something Beautiful That I Saw Today That Reminded Me Of You:

Today's Affirmation:

Everyday I Want To Say To You:

Everyday I Say To Myself:

I Sense:

I Know Today You Would Have Laughed At:

Today, My Moving Forward Plan Consisted Of:

I Am Being Filled

Date:

I Woke Up Feeling:

Biblical Scripture That Is Helping Me:

I Feel Better Knowing:

Your Life Has Taught Me:

Something Beautiful That I Saw
Today That Reminded Me Of You:

Today's Affirmation:

Everyday I Want To Say To You:

Everyday I Say To Myself:

I Sense:

I Know Today You Would Have
Laughed At:

Today, My Moving Forward Plan
Consisted Of:

I Am Being Filled

Date:

I Woke Up Feeling:

Biblical Scripture That Is Helping Me:

I Feel Better Knowing:

Your Life Has Taught Me:

Something Beautiful That I Saw
Today That Reminded Me Of You:

Today's Affirmation:

Everyday I Want To Say To You:

Everyday I Say To Myself:

I Sense:

I Know Today You Would Have
Laughed At:

Today, My Moving Forward Plan
Consisted Of:

I Am Being Filled

Date:

I Woke Up Feeling:

Biblical Scripture That Is Helping Me:

I Feel Better Knowing:

Your Life Has Taught Me:

Something Beautiful That I Saw
Today That Reminded Me Of You:

Today's Affirmation:

Everyday I Want To Say To You:

Everyday I Say To Myself:

I Sense:

I Know Today You Would Have
Laughed At:

Today, My Moving Forward Plan
Consisted Of:

I Am Being Filled

Date:

I Woke Up Feeling:

Biblical Scripture That Is Helping Me:

I Feel Better Knowing:

Your Life Has Taught Me:

Something Beautiful That I Saw
Today That Reminded Me Of You:

Today's Affirmation:

Everyday I Want To Say To You:

Everyday I Say To Myself:

I Sense:

I Know Today You Would Have
Laughed At:

Today, My Moving Forward Plan
Consisted Of:

Restoration Thoughts

Stay with me through my good and bad times.

I Am Being Filled

Date:

I Woke Up Feeling:

Biblical Scripture That Is Helping Me:

I Feel Better Knowing:

Your Life Has Taught Me:

Something Beautiful That I Saw
Today That Reminded Me Of You:

Today's Affirmation:

Everyday I Want To Say To You:

Everyday I Say To Myself:

I Sense:

I Know Today You Would Have
Laughed At:

Today, My Moving Forward Plan
Consisted Of:

I Am Being Filled

Date:

I Woke Up Feeling:

Biblical Scripture That Is Helping Me:

I Feel Better Knowing:

Your Life Has Taught Me:

Something Beautiful That I Saw Today That Reminded Me Of You:

Today's Affirmation:

Everyday I Want To Say To You:

Everyday I Say To Myself:

I Sense:

I Know Today You Would Have Laughed At:

Today, My Moving Forward Plan Consisted Of:

I Am Being Filled

Date:

I Woke Up Feeling:

Biblical Scripture That Is Helping Me:

I Feel Better Knowing:

Your Life Has Taught Me:

Something Beautiful That I Saw
Today That Reminded Me Of You:

Today's Affirmation:

Everyday I Want To Say To You:

Everyday I Say To Myself:

I Sense:

I Know Today You Would Have
Laughed At:

Today, My Moving Forward Plan
Consisted Of:

My poem to you....

I Am Being Filled

Date:

I Woke Up Feeling:

Biblical Scripture That Is Helping Me:

I Feel Better Knowing:

Your Life Has Taught Me:

Something Beautiful That I Saw
Today That Reminded Me Of You:

Today's Affirmation:

Everyday I Want To Say To You:

Everyday I Say To Myself:

I Sense:

I Know Today You Would Have
Laughed At:

Today, My Moving Forward Plan
Consisted Of:

I Am Being Filled

Date:

I Woke Up Feeling:

Biblical Scripture That Is Helping Me:

I Feel Better Knowing:

Your Life Has Taught Me:

Something Beautiful That I Saw
Today That Reminded Me Of You:

Today's Affirmation:

Everyday I Want To Say To You:

Everyday I Say To Myself:

I Sense:

I Know Today You Would Have
Laughed At:

Today, My Moving Forward Plan
Consisted Of:

Restoration Thoughts

I Am Being Filled

Date:

I Woke Up Feeling:

Biblical Scripture That Is Helping Me:

I Feel Better Knowing:

Your Life Has Taught Me:

Something Beautiful That I Saw
Today That Reminded Me Of You:

Today's Affirmation:

Everyday I Want To Say To You:

Everyday I Say To Myself:

I Sense:

I Know Today You Would Have
Laughed At:

Today, My Moving Forward Plan
Consisted Of:

I Am Being Filled

Date:

I Woke Up Feeling:

Biblical Scripture That Is Helping Me:

I Feel Better Knowing:

Your Life Has Taught Me:

Something Beautiful That I Saw
Today That Reminded Me Of You:

Today's Affirmation:

Everyday I Want To Say To You:

Everyday I Say To Myself:

I Sense:

I Know Today You Would Have
Laughed At:

Today, My Moving Forward Plan
Consisted Of:

I Am Being Filled

Date:

I Woke Up Feeling:

Biblical Scripture That Is Helping Me:

I Feel Better Knowing:

Your Life Has Taught Me:

Something Beautiful That I Saw
Today That Reminded Me Of You:

Today's Affirmation:

Everyday I Want To Say To You:

Everyday I Say To Myself:

I Sense:

I Know Today You Would Have
Laughed At:

Today, My Moving Forward Plan
Consisted Of:

I Am Being Filled

Date:

I Woke Up Feeling:

Biblical Scripture That Is Helping Me:

I Feel Better Knowing:

Your Life Has Taught Me:

Something Beautiful That I Saw
Today That Reminded Me Of You:

Today's Affirmation:

Everyday I Want To Say To You:

Everyday I Say To Myself:

I Sense:

I Know Today You Would Have
Laughed At:

Today, My Moving Forward Plan
Consisted Of:

It doesn't matter where you are, you will always be with me.

I know that you are in a space of love. I know that you are with God.

I know it's okay not to be okay. I also know it's okay to be okay.

I Am Being Filled

Date:

I Woke Up Feeling:

Biblical Scripture That Is Helping Me:

I Feel Better Knowing:

Your Life Has Taught Me:

Something Beautiful That I Saw
Today That Reminded Me Of You:

Today's Affirmation:

Everyday I Want To Say To You:

Everyday I Say To Myself:

I Sense:

I Know Today You Would Have
Laughed At:

Today, My Moving Forward Plan
Consisted Of:

I Am Being Filled

Date:

I Woke Up Feeling:

Biblical Scripture That Is Helping Me:

I Feel Better Knowing:

Your Life Has Taught Me:

Something Beautiful That I Saw
Today That Reminded Me Of You:

Today's Affirmation:

Everyday I Want To Say To You:

Everyday I Say To Myself:

I Sense:

I Know Today You Would Have
Laughed At:

Today, My Moving Forward Plan
Consisted Of:

I Am Being Filled

Date:

I Woke Up Feeling:

Biblical Scripture That Is Helping Me:

I Feel Better Knowing:

Your Life Has Taught Me:

Something Beautiful That I Saw
Today That Reminded Me Of You:

Today's Affirmation:

Everyday I Want To Say To You:

Everyday I Say To Myself:

I Sense:

I Know Today You Would Have
Laughed At:

Today, My Moving Forward Plan
Consisted Of:

I Am Being Filled

Date:

I Woke Up Feeling:

Biblical Scripture That Is Helping Me:

I Feel Better Knowing:

Your Life Has Taught Me:

Something Beautiful That I Saw
Today That Reminded Me Of You:

Today's Affirmation:

Everyday I Want To Say To You:

Everyday I Say To Myself:

I Sense:

I Know Today You Would Have
Laughed At:

Today, My Moving Forward Plan
Consisted Of:

Some things I have been doing to help others heal....

I Am Being Filled

Date:

I Woke Up Feeling:

Biblical Scripture That Is Helping Me:

I Feel Better Knowing:

Your Life Has Taught Me:

Something Beautiful That I Saw
Today That Reminded Me Of You:

Today's Affirmation:

Everyday I Want To Say To You:

Everyday I Say To Myself:

I Sense:

I Know Today You Would Have
Laughed At:

Today, My Moving Forward Plan
Consisted Of:

I Am Being Filled

Date:

I Woke Up Feeling:

Biblical Scripture That Is Helping Me:

I Feel Better Knowing:

Your Life Has Taught Me:

Something Beautiful That I Saw
Today That Reminded Me Of You:

Today's Affirmation:

Everyday I Want To Say To You:

Everyday I Say To Myself:

I Sense:

I Know Today You Would Have
Laughed At:

Today, My Moving Forward Plan
Consisted Of:

I Am Being Filled

Date:

I Woke Up Feeling:

Biblical Scripture That Is Helping Me:

I Feel Better Knowing:

Your Life Has Taught Me:

Something Beautiful That I Saw
Today That Reminded Me Of You:

Today's Affirmation:

Everyday I Want To Say To You:

Everyday I Say To Myself:

I Sense:

I Know Today You Would Have
Laughed At:

Today, My Moving Forward Plan
Consisted Of:

Restoration Thoughts

I Am Being Filled

Date:

I Woke Up Feeling:

Biblical Scripture That Is Helping Me:

I Feel Better Knowing:

Your Life Has Taught Me:

Something Beautiful That I Saw
Today That Reminded Me Of You:

Today's Affirmation:

Everyday I Want To Say To You:

Everyday I Say To Myself:

I Sense:

I Know Today You Would Have
Laughed At:

Today, My Moving Forward Plan
Consisted Of:

I Am Being Filled

Date:

I Woke Up Feeling:

Biblical Scripture That Is Helping Me:

I Feel Better Knowing:

Your Life Has Taught Me:

Something Beautiful That I Saw
Today That Reminded Me Of You:

Today's Affirmation:

Everyday I Want To Say To You:

Everyday I Say To Myself:

I Sense:

I Know Today You Would Have
Laughed At:

Today, My Moving Forward Plan
Consisted Of:

I Am Being Filled

Date:

I Woke Up Feeling:

Biblical Scripture That Is Helping Me:

I Feel Better Knowing:

Your Life Has Taught Me:

Something Beautiful That I Saw
Today That Reminded Me Of You:

Today's Affirmation:

Everyday I Want To Say To You:

Everyday I Say To Myself:

I Sense:

I Know Today You Would Have
Laughed At:

Today, My Moving Forward Plan
Consisted Of:

I Am Being Filled

Date:

I Woke Up Feeling:

Biblical Scripture That Is Helping Me:

I Feel Better Knowing:

Your Life Has Taught Me:

Something Beautiful That I Saw
Today That Reminded Me Of You:

Today's Affirmation:

Everyday I Want To Say To You:

Everyday I Say To Myself:

I Sense:

I Know Today You Would Have
Laughed At:

Today, My Moving Forward Plan
Consisted Of:

I Am Being Filled

Date:

I Woke Up Feeling:

Biblical Scripture That Is Helping Me:

I Feel Better Knowing:

Your Life Has Taught Me:

Something Beautiful That I Saw
Today That Reminded Me Of You:

Today's Affirmation:

Everyday I Want To Say To You:

Everyday I Say To Myself:

I Sense:

I Know Today You Would Have
Laughed At:

Today, My Moving Forward Plan
Consisted Of:

Seven daily scriptures that have helped me....

I Am Being Filled

Date:

I Woke Up Feeling:

Biblical Scripture That Is Helping Me:

I Feel Better Knowing:

Your Life Has Taught Me:

Something Beautiful That I Saw
Today That Reminded Me Of You:

Today's Affirmation:

Everyday I Want To Say To You:

Everyday I Say To Myself:

I Sense:

I Know Today You Would Have
Laughed At:

Today, My Moving Forward Plan
Consisted Of:

I Am Being Filled

Date:

I Woke Up Feeling:

Biblical Scripture That Is Helping Me:

I Feel Better Knowing:

Your Life Has Taught Me:

Something Beautiful That I Saw
Today That Reminded Me Of You:

Today's Affirmation:

Everyday I Want To Say To You:

Everyday I Say To Myself:

I Sense:

I Know Today You Would Have
Laughed At:

Today, My Moving Forward Plan
Consisted Of:

Fears I have about moving on....

I Am Being Filled

Date:

I Woke Up Feeling:

Biblical Scripture That Is Helping Me:

I Feel Better Knowing:

Your Life Has Taught Me:

Something Beautiful That I Saw
Today That Reminded Me Of You:

Today's Affirmation:

Everyday I Want To Say To You:

Everyday I Say To Myself:

I Sense:

I Know Today You Would Have
Laughed At:

Today, My Moving Forward Plan
Consisted Of:

I Am Being Filled

Date:

I Woke Up Feeling:

Biblical Scripture That Is Helping Me:

I Feel Better Knowing:

Your Life Has Taught Me:

Something Beautiful That I Saw
Today That Reminded Me Of You:

Today's Affirmation:

Everyday I Want To Say To You:

Everyday I Say To Myself:

I Sense:

I Know Today You Would Have
Laughed At:

Today, My Moving Forward Plan
Consisted Of:

I Am Being Filled

Date:

I Woke Up Feeling:

Biblical Scripture That Is Helping Me:

I Feel Better Knowing:

Your Life Has Taught Me:

Something Beautiful That I Saw
Today That Reminded Me Of You:

Today's Affirmation:

Everyday I Want To Say To You:

Everyday I Say To Myself:

I Sense:

I Know Today You Would Have
Laughed At:

Today, My Moving Forward Plan
Consisted Of:

I Am Being Filled

Date:

I Woke Up Feeling:

Biblical Scripture That Is Helping Me:

I Feel Better Knowing:

Your Life Has Taught Me:

Something Beautiful That I Saw Today That Reminded Me Of You:

Today's Affirmation:

Everyday I Want To Say To You:

Everyday I Say To Myself:

I Sense:

I Know Today You Would Have Laughed At:

Today, My Moving Forward Plan Consisted Of:

I Am Being Filled

Date:

I Woke Up Feeling:

Biblical Scripture That Is Helping Me:

I Feel Better Knowing:

Your Life Has Taught Me:

Something Beautiful That I Saw
Today That Reminded Me Of You:

Today's Affirmation:

Everyday I Want To Say To You:

Everyday I Say To Myself:

I Sense:

I Know Today You Would Have
Laughed At:

Today, My Moving Forward Plan
Consisted Of:

I Am Being Filled

Date:

I Woke Up Feeling:

Biblical Scripture That Is Helping Me:

I Feel Better Knowing:

Your Life Has Taught Me:

Something Beautiful That I Saw
Today That Reminded Me Of You:

Today's Affirmation:

Everyday I Want To Say To You:

Everyday I Say To Myself:

I Sense:

I Know Today You Would Have
Laughed At:

Today, My Moving Forward Plan
Consisted Of:

I Am Being Filled

Date:

I Woke Up Feeling:

Biblical Scripture That Is Helping Me:

I Feel Better Knowing:

Your Life Has Taught Me:

Something Beautiful That I Saw
Today That Reminded Me Of You:

Today's Affirmation:

Everyday I Want To Say To You:

Everyday I Say To Myself:

I Sense:

I Know Today You Would Have
Laughed At:

Today, My Moving Forward Plan
Consisted Of:

Restoration Thoughts

I Am Being Filled

Date:

I Woke Up Feeling:

Biblical Scripture That Is Helping Me:

I Feel Better Knowing:

Your Life Has Taught Me:

Something Beautiful That I Saw Today That Reminded Me Of You:

Today's Affirmation:

Everyday I Want To Say To You:

Everyday I Say To Myself:

I Sense:

I Know Today You Would Have Laughed At:

Today, My Moving Forward Plan Consisted Of:

I Am Being Filled

Date:

I Woke Up Feeling:

Biblical Scripture That Is Helping Me:

I Feel Better Knowing:

Your Life Has Taught Me:

Something Beautiful That I Saw
Today That Reminded Me Of You:

Today's Affirmation:

Everyday I Want To Say To You:

Everyday I Say To Myself:

I Sense:

I Know Today You Would Have
Laughed At:

Today, My Moving Forward Plan
Consisted Of:

I Am Being Filled

Date:

Today's Affirmation:

I Woke Up Feeling:

Everyday I Want To Say To You:

Biblical Scripture That Is Helping Me:

Everyday I Say To Myself:

I Feel Better Knowing:

I Sense:

Your Life Has Taught Me:

I Know Today You Would Have Laughed At:

Something Beautiful That I Saw Today That Reminded Me Of You:

Today, My Moving Forward Plan Consisted Of:

We are moving forward together. I know that God is with you.

38317229R00150

Made in the USA
Columbia, SC
05 December 2018